The Morning Muse

Mystical Revelations to Live By

The Morning Muse

Mystical Revelations to Live By

Octavia Williams

BOOKS

Winchester, UK
Washington, USA

First published by O-Books, 2016
O-Books is an imprint of John Hunt Publishing Ltd., Laurel House, Station Approach,
Alresford, Hants, SO24 9JH, UK
office1@jhpbooks.net
www.johnhuntpublishing.com

For distributor details and how to order please visit the 'Ordering' section
on our website.

ISBN: 978 1 78535 484 7
978 1 78535 485 4 (ebook)
Library of Congress Control Number: 2016936944

A CIP catalogue record for this book is available from the British Library.

Design: Lee Nash

Printed and bound by CPI Group (UK) Ltd, Croydon, CR0 4YY, UK

We operate a distinctive and ethical publishing philosophy in all
areas of our business, from our global network of authors to
production and worldwide distribution.

An economy of words is not a sign of unintelligence, but rather
a choice which knows that wisdom is inherent to the space between
the words.

The truest Truth is engaged with the Soul's sympathies, and will never be written at all.

Preface

This book is for those intent on realizing their True Nature, for those who would be empowered to live from Presence instead of person.

When used as a tool for transformation, it helps one on the pathless path to Self-Realization find the Truth for themselves through direct experience.

Right here and now, behind this visible world of sometimes good and sometimes bad, of sickness and health, war and peace, mounting success one year that only crumbles into failure another, exists a Reality beyond our wildest dreams; a Reality so stunning and perfect in its power and utter simplicity, that it needs no thought to sustain it and has no words to describe it.

The Morning Muse is a sharing and a gift of Love.

As part of the activity of the Center for Living Truth, it is a collection of spiritual revelations that have been coming through in meditation since December 2012 and e-mailed in the morning to those signed up to receive them.

This book of spiritual guidance and inspiration invites the serious seeker to discover not only their divinity, but the Master within. Comprising over 250 statements of Truth, it provides the missing link to living in the world, actually free of human lacks and limitations, and awakened from the illusion of separation from one's true Self. It can bring about life-changing results immediately. This is because the conscious awareness of Truth through one's own experience of Oneness breaks apart the mental constructs that have been holding beliefs, opinions and concepts in place, controlling life and obscuring Reality.

This book allows one to experience True Being, not just read about it. Knowing the letter of Truth is important, but ultimately does nothing just floating on the surface of our intellect. It must be assimilated into, dwelt with, tasted. More than words, we need enlightened understanding. We need to slow down, take our time, and realize it is the mind that wants the quick fix, the instant remedy. Revelation comes about in the absence of the time-mind and in the Silence behind the words.

Therefore, if taken into contemplation and allowed, the muse will unfold itself at deeper and ever expanding levels of Consciousness, bringing to Light the inherent Truth for any one individual at any one time.

The benefits are indescribable. But, if we are longing for spiritual transformation, we must be willing to live the Truth—to practice the principles consistently for them to work in our daily lives and bring about the harmony and fulfillment they promise. When we are an empty vessel, a clear channel, a transparency, the Kingdom of Heaven will open up and reveal Itself to be within the very Being that we are.

Once I began hearing from readers that "I save these you know," "I print them out" and "They're all over my house," I realized that in addition to what was happening in real time, a book was also being written. There are numerous testimonies to the timeliness, synchronicity and incredible helpfulness of the muses.

Open the book to any random page, meeting what you see with an open Consciousness. If the muse is read quietly, in the stillness of thought, and as the Silence of Soul, the Truth behind the words will speak what is meant for you to hear at that time.

And as with any book on spiritual Truth, don't ever take the author's word for what is being said. Don't accept what you read just because it seems to come from an outside authority. Go within, where the only real Authority is. If it resonates, if it "feels" true, that is your meter to determine its validity for you. These statements do not belong to an individual, but come from and go back to the One Consciousness.

My deep gratitude goes to Jeremy Stutsman and Peter Francis Dziuban for their generous time and encouragement, to my husband James, to the beautiful and ever-widening Circle of Light that are the recipients of the Morning Muse, and my little Olympus digital recorder, without which much of what came through could have been lost or forgotten.

Introduction

This is a book of reminders for anyone awakening to their True Identity. The seeming force of the world's outdated and erroneous beliefs and concepts, and their ability to capture our attention, needs to be met consciously with Truth and Silence.

This book is for those who are striving to live authentically, in harmony with their true nature, and who are willing and endeavoring to live beyond identification with thoughts and emotions and the duality that is the cause of all suffering. It is for those who have realized that they are not the body/mind, that their Essence is infinite and universal. It is for the one who knows the necessity of following through—whose sincere desire is for the inner individual unfoldment that enables the experience of Oneness as Reality.

Reality is experienced through a change in Consciousness, a change in perception. As Henry David Thoreau said, "It's not what you look at that matters—it's what you See." What we may not realize is that we are all mystics at heart, but conditioning through the ages has taught us to depend on teachers and writings outside of ourselves, when really, the true Master is within. We are what we have been searching for, and there is nothing outside of that. But we must do the work—no one can do it for us. We must go all the way...

Therefore, this is not as much a book for the mind, as it is for that part of us that is constant and unchanging. Every muse is a pointer that directs the attention within, whose words would awaken and enliven the Spirit.

But Truth Itself is not in the words. It is in the

4

Consciousness that brings forth the Word.

In being content with only an intellectual understanding, one misses the opportunity for the actual experience of Oneness with the Source of Being that can only happen through a pure Consciousness, when the mind is at rest. We don't need to know more Truth—we need to unknow the lie. We need more experiences of living as our true Self, in the Silence of that revelation.

We already are what we think we need to acquire; we have access to the wisdom of the ages, because it is the Substance of our very Being. As Christ Jesus said, "We are the Truth," and nothing in this so-called world of materiality can take that away from us.

Whether your background is in Buddhism, Hinduism, Advaita Vedante, Taoism, Sufism, Christian Science, The Infinite Way, A Course in Miracles, or any other orthodox religion or spiritual teaching, doesn't matter. These revelations come before any labels have been attached, thus speaking to the Heart of every Being. This is universal Truth and wisdom that one with an open and receptive Soul will hear.

Because there is only One Consciousness, One Mind, what is happening "here" is also happening "there." I learned very early on not to judge what came through, but to trust that each muse had a specific, ordained purpose and target that I knew not of, as attested to by the many responses I receive from those who share the divine synchronicity and timeliness of the particular muse for that day.

As the passing of time is illusory, however, these revelations are just as relevant now as when they came through.

Being timeless and infinite, Truth never stops expanding

and deepening as It is acknowledged, and It is not definitive. Each time a statement is gone back to, read and contemplated, it can bring about new meaning, insight and understanding.

And the miracle is that any one statement of It contains the whole of It, infinitely and eternally. It is a doorway into Silence, into the majesty of the unknown, into new Mansions, new aspects of Awareness where the teacher that is your own Being resides, where what is unique to you can be found, if you are willing to listen; if you are willing to open the door and walk through that threshold.

If we are to accept the Allness of God, we need to answer the call, fill the need, give when we're asked – because it is God calling. We must respond to Life as it is presenting Itself right now.

Fear is how we resist. It is a built-in mechanism of the ego created to hide the Truth from us. That uncomfortable feeling we get when we do resist what's happening right now is Spirit, the very Essence of ourselves, who we are, calling our attention to that fact – that we are not seeing the Truth of this present moment NOW.

There is no such thing as a future time when something is going to be impacted by what we do today. All of existence is right HERE and right NOW in all of its completeness and perfection. Fear and doubt and worry are things that exist only in the illusion of time.

*A*nd still... we must be watchful.
For the sense of a separate self to sneak in,
For awareness to wander away from Truth
and be caught in the net of illusion.

The minute there is an assignment of ownership – of
anything – we're out of Truth.

Consciousness is what Is,
and It is the One and undivided Self.

Consciousness knows that
there is only One Name – It is I.

There is gratitude from the One Heart
that It is always Being the Light of Truth,
the Light of Knowing –
It recognizes Itself.

And the gift that appears as belonging
to "another"
Belongs only to the One.

And the light that appears to be coming
from "another"
Abides Here, as the One Light that We Are.

*B*ehind any appearing visible form is the invisible, shining
Light of Living Truth.

*Our purpose is to shine that Light that we are. When we deny
the Light or refuse to surrender the darkness to It, we run
into trouble – our experience then seems to be full of
struggle, and disharmony starts to show up in the form of
illness, accidents and conflict.*

*The darkness disappears, when we see that it is not really
there in the first place.*

*W*hen we go into the Silence, we start with Infinity. We realize we are the everywhere, omnipresent, One Self already. If we sit with the belief that we are a separate self trying to meditate, trying to still our personal mind and then wait for God to impart some truth to us, we will always be waiting, because there are not two – us and God – there is only God.

We start with the All, as that is what we truly are. There is no becoming. There is no needing or wanting, because the All is fully Complete and Perfect, Infinite and Eternal. If that be so, then what could there be to need or want? We have it, because we are It.

Truth goes against everything we know, and the human mind will vehemently and aggressively try to resist it. It will say things to us like, "How can any of this be true? Look around you – there's no perfection. There's turmoil and hardship." It's going to tell us that Silence is boring, that meditation doesn't work.

But if we are to realize and experience Truth, our true nature, Oneness with our Source, we need to be aware of how obvious and subtle the ego can be, and that the testimony of the five senses is just that – it's what our five senses are telling us, and it can't be anything else – it doesn't have the capacity or the ability to be anything else.

During a walk on the Monticello trails,
but from beyond time and space, the Voice spoke to me...

Rest in the awareness of I AM,
abide there, live there, breathe there –
know that you're not really breathing,
Spirit is breathing you.

You're not walking,
God is walking as you.

Where the mind plays make-believe
with its world –
Life, Real Life, is beyond the masquerade, behind the images
of mental projection – before the mortal mask is put on.

Woods can stir the silent wonder
of the Soul.

We can't see through the illusion.

We can, however, recognize that Spirit
cannot see what isn't there,
and as our true identity is Spirit,
we must let go of the false identity of a separate me that sees
the illusion,
to correctly perceive Reality.

When we go within, and in the stillness
place our attention before the mind,
we witness right there,
the simple and yet Infinite Being
that we are.

*Beauty, is not something we see
out there with mortal eyes.*

*It's the Divine within us,
that we behold with Soul vision.*

*There is only
the enchantment
of this Eternal Moment.*

Thinking breaks the spell.

When we rise from material to spiritual Consciousness, it appears that we transcend, but really what we are doing is seeing the nothingness of the illusion.

As we acknowledge and accept the Truth, the lie dissolves, because Light and darkness cannot exist at the same time.

*G*ratitude is the acknowledgment that Only God Is Here.

When we go deeper than "us" and something we are thankful for, or content with – which is dualism – we see that True Gratitude is an acceptance of One Being – our Being – always fulfilling Itself as our Life.

Spiritually discerned, it is the acknowledgment that God is the source and substance of every seeming form, that it is infinite Presence, infinite Intelligence, and infinite Power. The more we hold this in our Consciousness, the more we live in the Grace that appears visibly as the need fulfilled.

*God speaks only when there is
no ego trying to talk.*

*If we want to hear the
Voice of Revelation,
we must slow down;
we must create the quietness,
the stillness and openness,
and retreat often from the
clang and clatter of the world.*

*Spirit is easy and gentle...
Spirit is Peace and Silence –
that still, small voice...*

Stillness is the founder of Heaven...

*When we take no thought,
human identity,
our false sense of self,
is automatically released –
revealing the already present stillness,
and there's no other place
where Peace resides.*

*Any Truth that appears to be revealed
from within "another" is within You.*

*There is only One Being, One Consciousness,
and that Consciousness is indivisible –
there is no separation.*

*I Am the Truth, I Am the Way –
look not for another.*

The (illusion of the) false prophet is within us, as all things are. The acceptance of and surrender to a person, place or thing as real is the giving away of the power of the Christ within, to the world mind to crucify.

It is that personal sense of self, the ego, that needs to be hung up on that cross.

*Tolerance is easy
when you realize
there is only One Self.*

You don't need to wait,
and you don't need permission:
Claim, your divinity right now.
Accept that you are the Allness of God.

There is not one concept in this world
that defines you.

ANY adversity appearing is but a gift –
a gift to take you higher
into the Consciousness of Now,
where Life is perfect and complete.

The Eternal Now is removed from passing time. Being in the Now is not being in this instant – this instant is a human concept in linear time.

Time is about sequence; Spirit is about simultaneity and spontaneity.

The awareness of Now, Is – pure in its simplicity, its sweetness and its power.

The body is God's viewpoint of Itself,
the focal point where
Consciousness can be seen.

Where you are visible is the evidence
of your invisible Eternal Being.

Living in Awareness

Between each thought and focus of
attention rests the Kingdom of Heaven
and our true identity as the King
of that Kingdom.

We only need to take no thought, and be still,
to realize the immediate Presence
that is always here, now,
in its finished perfection.

As morning dawns, and we awaken,
if we get still and withdraw our attention
from the personal sense of self,
we find ourSelves in the Light of Presence
that shines as a brand new day
with no memory, no mistakes –
no past, no future.

Every day like this is a testament to the
Eternal Now, and to the purity of the
clean, blank page on which that
Light of Presence shall write its perfect,
judgment-less, definition-less Book of Life.

We do not live in a house, a town or a country; we live in Consciousness,

and the more we let divine Truth be in that Consciousness, the more we find

that place we call home to be Heaven on Earth.

It is not until we realize we are nothing, that the Allness of God can establish Itself as the perfection of our Being.

Take no thought, and in that Silence,
listen to what the Heart is saying;
It is the compass of your Soul.

When we go into the silence to meditate we must remember
that it is not just a silence of sound and thought that we are
after; more importantly, it is the silence of the "personality"
in time and space.

Discipline is a gift of Grace that happens when we have made a full commitment towards the acceptance of, and the living in, the Love of our impersonal, infinite Self.

*A*ngels are the pure thought of God.

We have true humility when we can bow to the beggar, and hear wisdom from the wicked.

Remember not to reach for love
unaccounted for, in a person
(for where is he to be accounted of?)

Love is universal, not personal.

Only as we crucify the belief in a separate self, can the resurrection of our true Self in Oneness occur.

If you ever feel lost, or in the dark, give Love to something or someone. It is the surest and most direct way back into the Light of Being, where your true infinite and eternal Self is found – It will bring you Home.

In the illusion of the human scene, our needs and wants so carefully considered unwittingly obscure their very presentation as we wonder why they persist unfulfilled. If we are seeing in separation, a world of people, the "lucky ones" can tempt us to believe that only they shall prosper and see their dreams become real, while ours seem to wither like the petals of an orchid going dormant.

But who is there to be tempted, and who is it that is dreaming?

A life imperfect and incomplete exists only while we believe as such – that is its only power. What we accept, will be.

It may be easy to let go of the negative concepts we have about ourselves and about life, but we must let go of even the most positive ones as well, if we are to experience the magnificence of Reality in the Oneness of our Infinite Self.

We're not wrestling with demons –
only God, Consciousness, is Here.

That apparent conflict inside is our
divine immortal nature
that we are mistaking for
a separate mortal self.

It is trying to show us that the demons
are really angels in disguise.

Nothing Real can be seen outside the Light of Love.

Always start with Love, it is Home.

Freedom is seeing the universal nature of error – no pain, problem, or condition is ever localized. It only ever belongs to the nothingness of the world mesmerism from where it came.

Judgment is the jailer that keeps us locked up in the prison of belief in the power of effect.

There is only one Cause, and that is Love, and it is the expression of unconditional Love that breaks us free from the illusion of conditions.

Rest in the Silence of the Infinite
because that is all you are –
You are nothing more than That.

There is no separate self that needs to, or can become, illumined. There is only the One Infinite Light shining as every seeming individual point of Consciousness.

The degree to which we accept this Truth is the degree to which we will experience the reality of It.

It takes the constant surrendering of the concept of a personal sense of self, in Consciousness, to "experience" illumination.

*P*atience is easy when you know
and can trust in the completeness
and perfection of Now.

*When a problem, a discomfort, or even an annoyance,
comes into our awareness,
We don't react to it. We don't even respond to it.*

*We immediately pull our attention back from the situation
and be still.*

*We come before the mind to that inner Silence and wait. We
wait until that Peace descends that says, "All is well."*

*It isn't words necessarily, but a full, clear and deep peace – an
assurance, and a remembrance that, ah yes, this is the Truth.
It resonates with Soul, it feels right and true.*

*Whatever was bothering us then appears, as if by magic, to
disappear.*

*Consciousness is All, and it works to get our attention in
whatever way is right for us at any particular time.*

*Our reaction to what we think
are negative conditions "out there"
is what makes them persist.*

*What we are really seeing are
images in a mind
that we think belongs to us.*

*In Truth there is no becoming, anything,
only Being in this Perfect Now.*

Rest Now, in the stillness of My Love –
I am your breath,
I am the revealing,
this too shall fall away.

What troubles you cannot be saved,
and will seem to wither and disappear,
in My Radiance.

In meditation, we are not trying to achieve anything, including contact with Source, God.

We are not trying to reach a place of higher Consciousness where somehow more Truth will be imparted to us.

We are simply resting in the Silence of the Allness, the Omnipresence, Omniscience, and Omnipotence that We Are as Pure Consciousness.

Meditation is not a means to an end – it is an acceptance that Awareness is all that is Here and all that is Now.

*When you look for something,
you think it's not already there.*

The purpose of this visible world is to show us the degree to which we are One with the invisible. It is the outer evidence of the inner "attainment."

There is, of course, nothing to attain in the Perfection that we are, but it does appear that way to the human sense mind.

The visible is important, but remember, it is only the effect of our "attainment" or lack of it. It is the reflection of our Consciousness, and Consciousness is made of one Substance – as within, so without.

All of the intelligence "out there" in the whole history of the world is no match for one moment of Truth realized within.

Octavia Williams

*There is never anything wrong
except the belief that there is.*

Give this day to Omniscience – that which has nothing to do with a false, finite mind, but is the Infinite Intelligence that you are.

Don't think – Listen

Be Still and Know that I Am God
Consciously lived every day,
Is your Heaven on Earth.

There is nothing we need to do but rest
in the Silence of our Being,
in the knowing of our true identity,
in the stillness of our thought.

When we do this, we find that our world, our life, takes care
of Itself,
and the power of Grace in Oneness
reveals all to be Good.

Trust your Self – You Know

That which is boundless, limitless, dimensionless, direc-tionless, and yet beyond all definition, is what you are. It is the infinite awareness that is reading these words right now. It has no beginning, no end, and only exists here and now.

You Are That which is more intimate than knowing, for in the Experience, there's not even the knowing of That.

This appearing world of manifestation... is what is expressed as, but That is what you are – nobody living it, nobody knowing it. It cannot be known, It cannot be studied, it cannot be achieved – it cannot be lost, it cannot be found, it cannot be changed, it cannot be named. Forms are ideas (suggestions) that appear, and behind each form, whether animal, vegetable or mineral... That Alone Is – the life force that is the animating power behind all expression.

Nothing is required of you but to accept the Truth.

Whenever we feel something is too much, it's because it is. We have accepted a suggestion of otherness that weighs us down. Our true nature is Pure Consciousness – free and clear and light – simple, true.

The sense of heaviness is the burden of the lie, and a sign that our attention is not on, and that we are not living in, Truth.

In Truth, there are no problems – only opportunities to lift ourselves into a higher way of Seeing, out of a material awareness, into Spiritual Consciousness where all is Perfection, Now.

*D*arkness is the ignorance of Light.

The seeming "battle" between the Light of Truth and the darkness of ignorance will cease only when we stop pretending there is darkness – when we cease to recognize darkness, and accept that there is only Light.

Darkness eventually forces us to See the Light – that is its "soul" purpose.

In Reality, there is no dream that we must awaken from. For that to be true, there would first have to be a dreamer who is dreaming that dream. But no such separate identity exists – all there is, is Awareness, living Itself. The concept of a dreamer dreaming a dream, and then realizing that he must awaken from it, is a concept laid upon Pure Awareness which just Is.

Always make time in your day to simply sit, be still and surrender. Surrender everything – every idea and thought that you think you need. You don't need any of it, even thoughts of Truth. All you need to know is that you are the Child of God, and all will be well.

Whenever we see a problem,
no matter how small or insignificant,
we are declaring God impotent and
denying that He is running a perfect universe. Our experience
then is governed by the law of cause and effect instead of the
law of Grace.

*The lasting harmony
of all things in life
exists within the acceptance
that all there is, is Harmony.*

Truth in Consciousness is the only infallible immunity to the illusion of disease, and the only real infallible healer (revealer) there is.

*Who told you Life
was less than Perfect?*

*The sun is always rising
on this Eternal Day.*

When Love is unsolicited, it is the deepest and most true. If we allow ourselves to see beyond conditions to the pure and powerful Essence that is forever here, this Eternal Love that weaves the invisible fabric of Life in wonder and awe, that words cannot describe, that rights all wrongs and reveals the ever-existent Harmony and Perfection, we will witness this omnipotent Love as who and what we are, and never feel the need to ask, for anything, again.

IT IS THE SON OF GOD
that stands before you,
waiting to be recognized,
waiting to be acknowledged,
no matter what form is appearing
and no matter what that form is doing.

Speak only to Me...
and I will tell you
what you need to Hear.

Acknowledge only Me...
and I will show you
what you need to See.

*F*aith has nothing to do with a future,
but is a resting in the confidence of
the ever-present perfection of Now.

Genius is just the willingness to recognize and Be that white flame of inspiration that brings the beauty, power and harmony of the invisible, living Substance into visible manifestation.

It is the willingness to be persistent in perceiving that form is dying – it is not Creation, but a re-creation of Truth happening in time.

The Substance of Life is formless, and can only be accessed before the mind, through the timelessness of the Soul.

*E*verything you need, you have.

What you don't have, you don't need.

If we want to live as our True Self, we know we must surrender the false personal sense of self, but what we must make sure we are aware of is that only the Christ (our illumined awareness) can dissolve that illusion. The ego cannot, and would never, give up its (seeming) existence. It can't, because it in itself is part of the illusion, and of course, would never choose or be able to annihilate itself. It does seem to die hard though – putting up a fight every step of the way.

So if Spirit does the work of dissolving the illusion, then what are we to do? First, we Know that there is not Spirit and us – there is only Spirit. Then, we get still and create that vacuum of thought allowing for the omniscience and omnipotence of Illumination to experience Itself as us.

Only when we are living in and as our Spiritual Identity can the material world, including our sense of humanhood, be seen as the nothingness that it is. For Reality and illusion cannot exist at the same time and in the same place, and Light in our Consciousness reveals that darkness was never there.

Be still and Know... Be still and be free!

When you take no human thought, Divine Intelligence will direct your actions and speak through you. It will act from Love, and will protect you. In fact, our only real protection is our expression of Divine Love.

What you sow you will reap, meaning, what you believe is real will externalize and what you keep your attention on will become your experience. This is why it seems like sometimes we are "punished," and why "bad things happen to good people." We are outside the law and protection of Grace.

Of course there is never really anything to be protected from, but the human mind thinks so, because of its sense of separation and belief in evil.

*Y*ou can't get rid of what doesn't exist.

*If we are to be masters of our universe,
we must first be willing to be
the humble servants of Spirit.*

What we notice if we pay close attention is that the Way to awakening, the Way to freedom from lack and limitation, disease and discord is not through thinking. Thought is what creates this human world of bondage and when we live identified as a separate human being with its own mind, there is a misinterpretation of the Oneness that is really there.

The missing link to liberation is that the Truth must be recognized and accepted consciously within, and as, our Self.

It is important to know the letter of Truth, but the Way is not an intellectual process; it is in the Silence and trans-parency of mind that we un-believe this world of illusion, and experience
the world of Reality which is omnipresent, omnipotent, omniscient Consciousness.

Never give in to the temptation not to be original.

The fullness of Life is incomplete without your unique expression.

Imitation is suicide.

Why did Christ Jesus say to forgive seventy times seven? He knew that it is inevitable that the human mind will always be imperfect. It will make mistakes. It will love and then it will hate. It will speak truth and then it will lie, it will give and then it will take.

To live in our true identity as Christ Consciousness or illumined awareness, it is required of us that we constantly surrender our mortal beliefs and judgments, because that is the only way to attain the purity that is necessary for God to express, and bless, through us.

In Perfection, there is nothing to forgive.

As we become more and more aware of our true Identity, we must be careful not to associate with the image before us when we feel the Presence. We must be careful not to attach any person, place or thing to an experience of Oneness.

*Stand in the Truth – Refuse to accept anything other than
the wholeness of your Being.*

*There is nothing to do but Be. Like a stone pillar of peace and
serenity – stand still within, among the flying fragments of
the pairs of opposites – among the angels and demons of
human judgment that all seem to be "out there."*

*If you do, then each time the fires of tribulation burn, from
the ashes will rise and shine the clean, sparkling Light of a
brand new You in the brand new Day.*

When the world celebrates diversity, what's really happening is Spirit recognizing the commonality of Divine Essence behind the mask of human distinction.

Enlightenment is not something we attain – it's something we accept.

As separate human identities, we are powerless to do anything, to effect any outcome to bring about lasting harmony. But as we rest back in the One Infinite Self that is our true identity, in doing nothing, everything gets done.

We don't need to give in to the urge to control – God's got this!

The more you practice gratitude,
the more you open yourself up
to the abundance that is all around you.

What matters is the Light –
Light Sees only Love.

What matters is Love –
Love is Being Light.

How can we ever feel abandoned, when the very Essence that we are is divine omnipresence, omniscience, and omnipotence?

It only takes a moment to change our perception from little me to infinite I.

Love the illusion, and be grateful for it; it is not evil. God is all – and It is our Identity. It shows us how, through the pairs of opposites, to transcend the world of separation so that we may see and live in the reality of One Perfect Being.

Being Awareness and a separate me in time cannot happen simultaneously.

*There is no good, there is no evil,
there is only Perfection.*

*W*hen you live in the Invisible, the visible takes care
of itself.

The reason it seems we can't control our lives is that the lives we are trying to control don't really exist.

There is only one life that flows in Love, as Grace.

The more we are lifted into our immortal nature, the fainter our human footprints become, until the day we are conscious of soaring above this world of mortality, as our human stride is replaced with angel's wings.

One of the paradoxes of the mystical life is that we don't experience the immense power of Spirit until we slow down and withdraw our effort to do or be anything.

It must be realized that the moment we assume the false identity of a separate human being, we are power-less.

We have all the tools for transformation we will ever need right here, each day.

Every encounter, every experience has a lesson within it, or a Truth to be revealed, if we know to look and listen.

If it has an opposite, it isn't real.

*I Christ is the name,
and Perfection the activity,
of every individual we are aware of.*

Every discord is a summons to Silence.

Whenever an appearance of anything other than peace, joy, love, or beauty comes into our awareness, we transcend it by being still and instantly knowing the Truth of what is really there.

It's what we keep our attention on that becomes our experience. The less we listen to and act on the suggestions of world mind, the less frequently we will be suggested to. Our attention is all that keeps them alive – if we neglect to feed them, they will die of starvation.

There is only One Love, and It is not human or spiritual – It is beyond those distinctions.

It is an expression of Oneness based on Truth, not conditions.

The greatest blessing we can give is to be true to our highest revelation.

Are we living by chance or by certainty?

Acting on any finite concept presented to our awareness by collective world thought is not only unreliable, it is a limitation of ourSelf and our experience of Oneness.

But if we act from the place of no thought, we will be living in, and thus can rely on, the Infinite, which is always guiding and directing harmoniously and perfectly.

Never, ever accept a limitation, even if it has been going on for 50 years – it is a lie. We cannot be complacent about what the senses report. All that is really there where the imperfection seems to be is infinite and eternal Wholeness, unbound by time or space.

*Our only real strength
is in knowing our true Identity.*

As we ascend into fuller and fuller realization of Being, we will be tempted in the areas of our life where our conviction of the Truth is the weakest.

Our function, then, is to stand fast in the Living Light of Truth, constantly being aware enough to recognize the inevitable suggestions that will try to cause us to waver.

This Light, that we are, will always gently illumine the dark corners of our Consciousness, to show us where we have been withholding Love.

Rest in the Truth,
then let the Silence respond.

*W*ords are necessary only when we are not hearing the Word, and make themselves obsolete as we listen within.

Impersonalize that condition that appears to be imperfect, and realize there is no cause or substance to sustain it.

Anything that appears inharmonious must be instantly seen as a mirage – merely a collection of thoughts and mental images that have nothing whatsoever to do with You.

Believing what you see is the only way it can seem to be real, and the only reason it will seem to persist.

*H*ave faith in Me, not the things of this world, for I will
never leave you nor forsake you. Your only security lies not
with your employer nor your doctor, but in your continuous,
conscious awareness that You and I are One.

*Hope assumes that there is something
that is not Whole, Complete
and Perfect right now.*

*L*ove your adversary –
it is your Savior in disguise.

I am the only Presence,
the only Power,
the only Knower.

What is revelation,
but the recognition of the One Self.

*Don't ever fight against what is –
it is the way it is, for a reason.*

Not only are you a unique expression of the Infinite, but you are absolutely essential to the Divine Plan.

*The Deep Silence of My Peace
is the only Awareness that reveals the
Truth of Perfection.*

*A*dversity is sometimes the call to come out
of complacency.

*The potent combination of an intense longing
to Know our True Nature
and the willingness to open our
Consciousness to the Infinite,*

brings about transformation –

*but nothing will happen,
unless nothing else matters.*

Soul sees no obstacles.

If we find we are coming up against something limited in some way, whether it be in the form of a firmly held belief, or a fleeting thought, we must recognize that it is world mind tempting us away from our infinite nature, where of course the possibilities are endless.

As soon as we get back into our true Identity, the one right way will become apparent, and the barriers will lift.

*If we ever feel like God has abandoned us,
we must remember, it is the other way around –
we have abandoned our Identity
as the Infinite, Living Spirit of God.*

The illusion, is that we see with two human eyes.

The Reality, is that we see through the One I of our Being, with Perfect, Infinite Vision.

Futility is another way Life has of getting us to turn within – to let go of our ways, and surrender to the One Way.

At any moment, we can rest in the stillness and turn away from the logic and reason of world thought, to the infinite intelligence that is continuously operating as the I of our Being.

*The deeper our humility,
the greater our capacity
for the Infinite.*

What is before us is what has been given us to do.

To fully live in Truth, we must continuously surrender all that we know – even those concepts of Truth that are the most comforting, for the real Comforter must be unknown and unseen. The real Comforter is the conscious realization Now, of our true identity as Infinite Awareness.

The only real resurrection is the stepping out of the tomb of passing time, when we recognize and accept that there is no Life, Power, Beauty, Harmony, Substance, Eternality, or Immortality, in any kind of belief of a future or a past.

Only God is Now, and Only Now is God.

Be attentive,
for what you accept in "another"
you will experience yourself,

for Oneness is real
and separation an illusion.

The stories that tempt us back into time
and to a false need for belonging,
will dance and sparkle forever,
until it is recognized that we are that
Immortal Self they will never know.

Everything we would be anxious about is already in perfect order within the Divine Plan.

Worry is waste.

If God is All, then who is the adversary? And what is world mind?

Be not afraid, it is I.

Spirit must sometimes disguise Itself as the adversary, and needle us, until we realize that the "problem" isn't really there.

This is so the One can gather up all the seemingly separate parts of Itself back into the realization of its Oneness.

How else could the illusion be broken? How else could we rouse ourselves from this deep sleep of hypnotism, if everything is going well? We would continue to sleep...

Problems, discords of any kind, are there to awaken us from the dream of separation, so we can live again, truly whole, complete and perfect.

An enemy is only an image believed to be "out there."

Bring it closer in – there must be distance for fear to function.

Unless we invite the invisible Essence behind the images back, we are in denial of our Wholeness and Allness.

Whether the perceived enemy is person or condition,

Bring it closer in, and see how much it looks like You.

Nothing can hurt us while in our embrace.

When it is said, we have Eternal life, what does that really mean?

Eternity has not just to do with an infinite forever, but is a fullness and completeness that contains the past, the present and the future, simultaneously.

The more we live in the Christ,
the more we see God's work being done.

The most "successful" Truth student will be guided only by their inner Teacher, who shows that in Reality, there is no success or failure, and there is no student or teacher.

All is one heavenly Experience that is complete at any given moment.

Fear is only the ignorance that Love is all that is ever expressing.

*T*he only way Grace can seem to not be functioning in Life,

is if there is no conscious awareness of its Ever-Presence.

*The walls of any seeming prison
are the false beliefs and misinterpretation
of an illusory, human mind.*

We cannot expect to experience the Allness of the Infinite unless and until we accept that that is all we are.

Sense mesmerism can be strong and stubborn, but our knowing the Truth of One Power renders it impotent.

If this moment seems lacking in anything, it is because we have dropped down into a false human consciousness where there is always incompleteness and imperfection. Any attempt to judge will only bring more insufficiency.

Never want anything more or less. Omnipresence is ever-perfect and always sufficient.

Live as this Grace, and things you didn't even know you needed will be added unto you.

The Power is within You, and nowhere else.

What you keep your attention on shows forth in your experience, and will seem to increase the more you focus on it.

In Grace there is patience, as patience forces us to keep our attention centered in Now.

The constant practice of living in Truth eventually leads to the Experience taking over, and the Truth living You.

Bless your "problems."

They are what keep you from being satisfied with your life, and what cause you to reach deeper for Truth.

It is the depth of the conviction of the truth of our Identity that determines the height of our Awareness.

Catch the fact that matter
is a mental concept
and watch the disharmony dissolve.

There is no depth of Truth as deep as the complete opening to the fullness and perfection of Life, that is right here and that is right now.

We can so easily postpone the inevitable, by thinking we have to wait for something to appear visibly that is already there invisibly. Can we accept, that in any divinely ordained activity, we are given all that we ever need, every step of the way?

Waiting just postpones the inevitable. Trust the paradoxes of this path. They never make logical sense, and that's the point – they're not supposed to.

We won't see the Reality of a person, place, thing, condition or situation unless and until we see its Beauty.

*F*ollow the invisible impulse within, without letting the mind tell you why you're doing it.

What has that to do with Me?

Love and Perfection is all that is Here.

*L*et

The question would never be asked
if the answer were not already known.

Don't get caught off guard.

*There is only the Light – living, moving
and having its Being in the
Oneness of Love.*

It's the illusory human ego that when misperceiving the apparent strength in an apparent other person, allows itself to feel weak.

Real strength and power comes from Knowing that the Self of you and the Self of another is the same One Self, with nothing to oppose it.

Be still, and Listen.

What does Love have to say
to You today?

A *separate sense of self can arise only when we have become separated from Now.*

If it doesn't include all, it isn't Oneness.

*If we're not standing in the Truth,
we're standing in the way.*

*The Infinite cannot express
where It is not recognized.*

*E*very moment is a Holy Moment
whether we feel the Reverence or not –
we are always being Blessed.

*Divine direction always contains
a peace, an ease, a gentle flow
that when awakened to,
feels like it's always been flowing.*

The reason we seem to suffer and struggle is that we are One Infinite Being trying to live as many human beings. How can one have control over a human life that does not exist? You don't need to figure it out – just rest in the Silence of your infinite identity, and let Omniscience work through you.

I give up – I give over to the Source of Being, my life. As a separate human being I know I can do nothing, because in truth, there is no such thing – Oneness is real, and is all that is real. This is why I choose to surrender, to live in eternal wholeness and harmony, not in temporary separation. The fewer human footsteps I take, the more capacity there is for the realization of my divine nature.

Give every moment to God, and eternal Glory will be given.

Our real employment is to create Heaven on Earth – through our words, our deeds, our talent and our Vision. It can only be brought about by the Love we allow to express through us.

All any great endeavor requires is the relinquishing of a separate self that would try to accomplish it.

Only the Pure in Heart shall Know God.

Know that – your Temple is already cleansed.

Ownership is a yoke that keeps us tethered to a seeming world of illusion, but in the acceptance of our Allness, we can realize the Truth.

There is nothing quite as freeing as relinquishing ownership.

Be the Christ, see the Christ,
release the Christ...

Nothing is ever lost that cannot be found, if we simply change our perception.

As we look through spiritual vision, there we observe Perfection – everything is as, and where, it should be.

Can we let go of good enough, for out-of-this-world magnificence?

We are not meant to settle for an ordinary Life. Our true existence and experience is a Life so extraordinary, it is beyond our wildest dreams.

There is no substitute for Silence.

The masters that seem to be out there in forms called people or writings are merely an imitation of the Real Teacher that is your pure, infinite Being. Ultimately, the Master you seek is within.

There is no substitute for Silence, and if we want to be aware of Oneness, we must become unaware of the duality of humanhood. They cannot co-exist.

The miracle is that not only are you a unique expression of the One Divine Consciousness, but your individuality is Infinite.

When one trial after another seems to be turning into a
perfect storm of inharmony that threatens to blow us off
course, if we can rise in Consciousness to what really is –
Infinite Love Now – we'll see that none of it is "out there."
It is only in the beliefs that we have accepted, that are
trying to tempt us out of Reality.

Awaken now,

to what this blessing brings

and the wind will be nothing

but a thousand angel's wings.

We create our own darkness by not allowing the Light that is our very Essence to shine, to illuminate those dark places that are nothing more than our resistance to this Light.

There are no shadows unless something is blocking the Light.

Many times, an appearance of lack is only an emptying out of something old and unnecessary – embrace it, and a new, fuller expression of Life will soon replace it abundantly.

*E*ven *if we seem inconsistent, we must flow with Life and be willing to go wherever it takes us – literally and figuratively.*

Any obstacle can be "overcome" if we are willing to accept that it is not really there.

Let the Realization arise – embrace it, embody it, but then let it fall back into the no-thing-ness from which it came. Don't try to keep it, for it is not of time – it comes from outside of time, and is only for the moment that it comes.

Its purpose is not to remain – its purpose is to take you higher.

Don't ever be concerned that your social circle is shrinking – that old friends and certain family members are falling away. For it means that you are doing the work, and realizing the spiritual household of which you are always a member.

A circle of friends is no substitute for the Circle of Christ.

Nothing is outside of Consciousness.

The appearance of a persistent problem only shows us that we are not persistently knowing the Truth about it. We must not treat any seeming disturbance as if it were something separate from and outside of ourSelf, but recognize that our belief that it is real and separate is the only problem. A thought is just a thought – it has only the power that our attention gives it.

Thank any appearance for showing you what is really there, and the green will turn to Gold.

*Resisting what's unwanted
only gives that lie a longer life.*

The mind is not the enemy, just the vessel by which the Heart pours forth its Love into expression, the Truth it Knows, which can only be done when it is transparent and clear – not polluted with a "me" sense.

Only still waters can reflect an undistorted image.

Is there someone separate from us who is doing something wrong, or is it we who have not washed the mud off the diamond?

Love your enemy, for it is only your closest friend asking you to take off its mask.

What the Heart doesn't approve is folly, and need never waste your time.

Love alone knows the difference between the imitation and the Real.

Acceptance is the solvent that dissolves the sense of conditioned matter. The more we accept the Truth of Being, the more we will experience that Radiant, Light of Being – that Luminosity that is other-worldly.

To the degree that our attention is not centered in the
Truth *of Being is the degree that we are hypnotized. Living
in Truth, as we are aware of it, requires a constant
vigilance until the abiding is automatic.*

Persistence is the secret to any successful practice.

Each day, we come into new Light, as old ways are falling away. If we're finding what worked before no longer does, it's time to trust the untried and the unknown.

Serenity says, I Am what's Real in the midst of the appearance of the pain, the rage or the chaos.

All Love asks is that we see Life Its way – that nothing has to be a burden, that no one has to cry, that the pieces that seem to be broken are really just completed Creation in slow motion – drawn out by time. Stay strong in the knowledge that Love, always, sees us through.

*Realizing our innate Purity requires that we be humble
enough and brave enough to admit when we are not
accepting the Truth of a particular condition or situation.*

Awakening is an activity of Love, that is done by, for, with and because of Love.

And it doesn't end with the realization of Oneness. It is as if we are living in a foreign country – we must become translators of Truth, actively translating everything that comes into our awareness – the lies, duality, and even half-truths – into the fullest and most total Truth that we know.

Seeing through the visible appearance to what's really there – the invisible Christ – is how Reality externalizes in our Life.

You are a Masterpiece, a divine Revelation of the most brilliant Idea the Infinite ever had.

Never assume you are supposed to do anything in Life, big or small, that doesn't come easily, naturally, and with a great Love and Joy.

Disregard the suggestions that might come to tempt you to judge or compare.

The seeming dis-ease is never in the "body" – it is in the belief that a separate body exists.

It is in your Consciousness, and Truth can only be revealed through a change in that Consciousness.

Be still and Know, as often as it takes, that My Peace is the great revealer of Truth – the manifestation of Wholeness and Perfection.

Dare to accept your Divinity. The identity you think you will lose was never real and was never yours to begin with.

Don't ever let the opinion of "another" overrule the inner Knowing of your Heart.

What feels right, is right.

Resist not the thing that troubles you. If you fall into it, you will find that you fall through it, because it is not really there. It is then that the Peace that passes understanding will descend.

Dwell in this Peace for as long as you can, for It is . what makes all things New.

The fastest way to get somewhere is to know you have already arrived – in Reality, there is nowhere to go because everywhere is Here.

Distance is but a concept created by a sense of separation.

As we expand in Consciousness, we become much more sensitive and aware. Many of us find that things that used to bother us don't anymore, but to our surprise, things that we never took notice of now seemingly have the ability to tempt us to react.

If we are not aware of what is going on, we can be tempted to think we are not progressing, or have slipped back. The opposite is true. We are being fine-tuned and prepared for transition into Christ Consciousness. We are being asked to transmute these illusions and see them for what they really are – Divine Essence, not conditioned matter.

Your True Body is a Temple of Light that is infinite and eternal, and this mental imitation we call a "world" is nothing but a collection of thoughts and beliefs in separation from this Light. And that is the Truth of every so-called form you become aware of.

Exclusion of anyone or anything as this Light, in Consciousness, prevents it from actualizing as your Experience.

There is a fire burning within that contains our True Purpose. It doesn't make the distinction between outer and inner, and it doesn't know how to do anything but burn. If withheld, it will consume us – but if released, will transform our Life.

This fire is Love, and it is our Identity.

In Now, we need take no thought – thinking interrupts the natural flow of Life, in Perfection and Completeness. If we live in time, we will always be trying to do something or get somewhere. Living outside the time that seems to be passing, we experience "It is done." There is nothing that isn't Finished, and there is nowhere but Here, no matter what the images of this world, including our bodies, seem to be saying or doing.

Recognize that you live in the completeness of Now that is always, continuously, and you will never know lack.

Standing in the Truth of Oneness without habit or direction, not needing routine or prediction, is facing each day confidently knowing that we don't know what's going to happen, but neither do we need to know. Because when the Light of Being is living our Life as Us – It Knows, and that's enough.

Be not afraid, it is I.

The I can never leave, nor forsake you, because I Am is the very essence of your Being. It matters not how great or small the discord appears to be – refuse to see it. The Light of wholeness, harmony and abundance can only shine through when Consciousness is pure and unobstructed by false belief.

Be not afraid, it is I.

That which we feel most resistant to doing, is that which we most need to do.

Know there is no personal doer, and the river of Right Activity will flow unobstructed.

*The mental noise of world thought decreases as we
lose interest in the story.*

It is our attention, that is the Power, as it animates and brings Life to whatever it is we are focused on.

Watch what you are concentrating on...

When we stand convicted in One Light, One Presence, One Power, suggestions (if they come at all) of anything other than pure Love and Harmony dissolve like snowflakes on a flame.

Peace can only come with surrender.

Grace is an acceptance of, and a letting of, whatever needs to happen, happen. To love and trust the Infinite so much, that we're willing to, and find the strength to, secede.

Grace is the surrender of control, of anything. In doing nothing, we become the beholder of everything that needs to get done, being done.

In Grace, Peace and unspeakable Joy in the expanse of Infinity awaits us.

To live without expectation is to experience more than what we would expect.

It is to find that what is divinely here and now, in all its complete and perfect fulfillment, always exceeds our expectations.

You are unlimited – and that will be your experience to the extent that you are open and receptive and willing to drop words like can't, won't and shouldn't from your vocabulary.

*Never fear intellectual emptiness –
it is a natural sign of Grace, preparing the vessel
for spontaneous divine fulfillment, divine
omniscience, Now.*

*The one who knows nothing is Everything. Wisdom is
what springs forth from the emptiness when one has
accepted their true nature.*

The more we know there is no actual law to sustain an illusion of discord, the sooner we will see that discord dissolve.

God governs Itself in Love and Justice, Purity and Perfection.

After you know the Truth, you must completely unknow the Truth for it to become a living Experience.

Only in the absence of "human" thought can Divine Intelligence operate.

The solution is contained in the closest, most obvious thing to us. It's never something obscure or far away in either time or space. It is never hidden nor does it need to be figured out (that would involve thinking, and the Infinite operates above the level of mind). If we are open to accepting this Truth, we find it within our Awareness.

This is what is meant by "Thy Grace is my sufficiency."

We can do nothing of ourselves, because there is no human self. This is It, we are It – the embodiment of God, here and now, as we are, independent of identification with human thought. It's so ridiculously simple and obvious, that we miss it.

Recognize I as a living Experience.

Everything we see in this world is but mental effect, with no power, substance, Reality or law to sustain it. The only power is in what we accept, because we are original Cause. We are the infinite, invisible, living Light.

Does God need a reason to exist? Do we need a reason to explain why we're alive or what we're doing in Life? No. If we are about the Father's business, we listen to, and we act from the divine impulse within, with no reasoning and no explanation necessary.

You cannot fit the Infinite into any sort of finite frame. When we unsee the mental constructs that have been erected, they of course will vanish. They were only there to the judgment of an imaginary, separated self.

Do what you do because it feels loving and free. Let it rest there – don't let the mind adulterate it.

Thoughts have no power, substance, intelligence or law to sustain them. They are a mental mirage.

The conscious awareness of the Infinite Invisible Reality of God is the Is-ness that needs neither power nor wisdom.

The paradox of a possibly inconvenient Truth is that our commitment to Truth will not make our human life better – it will rip that human life apart, for the sake of, and in the name of, My Peace.

It accepts nothing less than the total Perfection of everything we are aware of, Now, as it reveals the nothingness of a so-called material world.

The most special "times" and "places" are those when and where the veil has parted, and we have become aware of the Eternal Now which is the Divine.

The suggestion says, "You have to do something about this." But hear Spirit's whisper, "Be still, hush."

There is an immense freedom in not judging, because you know that nothing in "this world" really matters.

The more we live in and depend on our infinite spiritual Body, the more it will respond to us.

The great secret is to trust only the Infinite Invisible.

This is practicing the Absolute, this is living in our Allness.

A harmonious Life is like a river that is constantly flowing...

We dam it up by holding on to concepts of what that should look like. If we want our experience to be one of Peace and Joy, we must loosen our grip.

Let it go, let it go, let it go – let everything go, until the day we can have enough faith and trust to not grab a hold of anything.

Honor everything that happens – it is necessary for your unfoldment. Allowing the mind to judge or resist dishonors Grace, and inhibits the expression and manifestation of Its natural flow.

Don't let the mind judge what it knows nothing about.

In Reality, what appears as giving is merely an allowance of the expression of Fullness to come forth.

You can't give to or take away from that which is already Complete.

Fear not, what looks like tragedy, whether "personal" or "global", may only be the constructs of the old matrix breaking apart in order that Harmony and Perfection be seen in its place.

That which appears to be wrong will never change until our Consciousness of it changes, because they are one and the same.

Perception is manifestation.

We must be spiritual warriors choosing silence and stillness as our only weapons against any so-called "enemy," whatever form that enemy takes. In Reality, it makes no difference.

In wielding the sword of Truth, we're choosing to continuously accept only the allness of Perfection.

Surrender to and shine the Light within – Smile.

If we spend most of our day in the darkness of human belief, we cannot expect Illumination. The Light does not come "down to where we are" – we must reach for it with divine longing in the recognition of the Truth of our identity as It.

Miracles are witnessed when we surrender everything to the Light.

The mountain that we think we must climb to be at the top of, in order to Know the Truth of our Being, is a mental mirage. The "path of Ascension" is not a horizontal one, but it is also not a vertical one. In Reality, there is no dimension or direction – or path.

It is a conscious choice to constantly stay awake to the Truth, to live in the Truth, Now. By doing so, old beliefs dissolve, and Grace is there in all its monumental glory.

All the world wants to wallow in its misery, and wants us to wallow with it.

Once we awaken to Truth, we are a wayshower who then has the ability and the responsibility to lead those who think they have been blinded to the Light.

By stepping up and choosing to acknowledge One Presence and One Presence only, continually, any darkness in our world disappears in the Light of True Identity.

Never own what seems to be wrong or right – it can only be so to an assumed, false human identity. The problem is never yours, nor is any accomplishment. Impersonalize, impersonalize, impersonalize. Never accept anything as belonging to you. The only You there is, is the possession-less Allness of pure and radiant Love.

Nothing comes into our awareness purposeless, and it is all our Consciousness in which nothing exists outside of.

Life is an endless teaching... if we're paying attention...

*J*ust...

Now

*Have faith that as you dwell in your invisible Identity
your visible experience will take care of itself, that
Divine Order is always functioning, perfectly. Let go of
who you think you are, and what you think you should
be doing and trust that the Infinite Invisible knows
how to live Its Life as You.*

*Your need is not so much to understand with the mind,
but to accept with the Heart.*

Where it's hardest for us to Love is where we need to Love the hardest.

*E*njoy the fullness of Life, every aspect of it that is available now – nothing ever needs to be saved for later, for there is no shortage in Infinity and there is no time but Now.

Take no thought,

and let Love flow...

Transformation never comes about by playing it safe.

We must go to the edge of our comfort zone, and leap!

Divine discontent is the only malady we can ever really suffer from, and being content with God Al-one is its only remedy.

*T*he veil of illusion is only ever a thought held tightly
in your grasp.

*Release your grip, and everything in life will start
loosening up.*

The practice is not to ignore this visible world, but to keep looking past it, beyond it, to its invisible Source. If God is All, then It is everywhere and everything – infinitely. If we keep looking, we soon discover the Essence of Life, and what our senses perceive, to be One Divine Substance.

Keep Looking...

Conditioned life lives in a groove of repetition and predictability – stuck in patterns with only the slightest variations day to day, week to week. In fact, it is really not life at all, but an imitation of life that is as "dead as a door nail." If this is ever our experience, it is because we are entertaining material, finite beliefs in separation that are clouding our perception, causing us to see from a most limited perspective. We're not living out from Reality, the Reality of Pure Essence, Infinite Being, which is always new, always spontaneous, and infinitely varied.

The Everpresent Truth (that we are) lies dormant until It is activated by our recognition, acknowledgment and acceptance of It.

We activate Its power by doing nothing but getting so still, that in the womb of Silence, It is allowed to be birthed in our Consciousness.

Don't be afraid to take a holiday from living with expectation, whether "yours" or "another's." You don't have to do anything you don't want to.

Shoulds are lies that hide the Right Action that would reveal Harmony.

The greatest gift we can bring is the willingness to accept the Christ identity of those who appear to be doing wrong.

This is the true majesty of living in the Kingdom.

*It is in our humbleness
that we are exalted.*

Love is all that is ever expressing, waiting patiently
Here for a channel to express through. The question to
ask is, what are we holding onto that is blocking
this flow?

It is not the person, seemingly out there, we are seeing
as imperfect, but the concept of them we are carrying.
If we can drop that weight, we will "rise" to a finer,
subtler Consciousness of Light and Perfection.
Disease, discord and disharmony of any kind is nothing
more than the result of the flow being blocked.

The knowing of this outshines and dispels the ignorance
of any erroneous suggestion.

We don't need to rely on the mind to remember, but on the Heart that always Knows what to say, what to do, and who and what It is. Drawing forth from the Infinite Unknown, It speaks immediately and spontaneously from the Eternal Now. The five-sense mind can only speak from what it knows, as it can only draw from its finite conditioning of feedback from the brain.

O! the grand paradox of realizing that true Intelligence can never come from thinking, but is only available through the Love of an open Heart.

Those who seek, will find.

Those who accept, will Be.

In the end, we have no choice really, but to follow where Love leads – to be obedient to that great and gentle Force within.

Thank you for purchasing *The Morning Muse – Mystical Revelations to Live By*. For further interest and to reach Octavia, please visit the Center for Living Truth website for contact info, news on upcoming events, recent blog posts and to sign up to receive the Morning Muse:

http://www.centerforlivingtruth.com.

The Center for Living Truth supports the awakening individual with practical tools for living an authentic life in and as the truth of Being. It provides resources and direction for the mystical journey Home, as well as a spiritual community of support where all can share in the unfolding of Consciousness. It is a gathering place for study, meditation and conscious conversation, creating an opportunity for the experience of illumination and the direct knowing of ourselves as Pure Awareness.

BOOKS

O-BOOKS

SPIRITUALITY

O is a symbol of the world, of oneness and unity; this eye
represents knowledge and insight. We publish titles on
general spirituality and living a spiritual life. We aim to
inform and help you on your own journey in this life.
If you have enjoyed this book, why not tell other readers by
posting a review on your preferred book site?
Recent bestsellers from O-Books are:

Heart of Tantric Sex
Diana Richardson
Revealing Eastern secrets of deep love and intimacy to
Western couples.
Paperback: 978-1-90381-637-0 ebook: 978-1-84694-637-0

Crystal Prescriptions
The A-Z guide to over 1,200 symptoms and their healing
crystals
Judy Hall
The first in the popular series of four books, this handy little
guide is packed as tight as a pill-bottle with crystal remedies
for ailments.
Paperback: 978-1-90504-740-6 ebook: 978-1-84694-629-5

Rising in Love
My Wild and Crazy Ride to Here and Now, with Amma, the
Hugging Saint
Ram Das Batchelder
Rising in Love conveys an author's extraordinary journey of
spiritual awakening with the Guru, Amma.
Paperback: 978-1-78279-687-9 ebook: 978-1-78279-686-2

Thinker's Guide to God
Peter Vardy
An introduction to key issues in the philosophy of religion.
Paperback: 978-1-90381-622-6

Your Simple Path
Find happiness in every step
Ian Tucker
A guide to helping us reconnect with what is really important
in our lives.
Paperback: 978-1-78279-349-6 ebook: 978-1-78279-348-9

365 Days of Wisdom
Daily Messages To Inspire You Through The Year
Dadi Janki
Daily messages which cool the mind, warm the heart and
guide you along your journey.
Paperback: 978-1-84694-863-3 ebook: 978-1-84694-864-0

Body of Wisdom
Women's Spiritual Power and How it Serves
Hilary Hart
Bringing together the dreams and experiences of women

across the world with today's most visionary spiritual
teachers.
Paperback: 978-1-78099-696-7 ebook: 978-1-78099-695-0

Dying to Be Free
From Enforced Secrecy to Near Death to True Transformation
Hannah Robinson
After an unexpected accident and near-death experience,
Hannah Robinson found herself radically transforming her
life, while a remarkable new insight altered her relationship
with her father; a practising Catholic priest.
Paperback: 978-1-78535-254-6 ebook: 978-1-78535-255-3

The Ecology of the Soul
A Manual of Peace, Power and Personal Growth for Real
People in the Real World
Aidan Walker
Balance your own inner Ecology of the Soul to regain your
natural state of peace, power and wellbeing.
Paperback: 978-1-78279-850-7 ebook: 978-1-78279-849-1

Readers of ebooks can buy or view any of these bestsellers
by clicking on the live link in the title. Most titles are
published in paperback and as an ebook. Paperbacks are
available in traditional bookshops. Both print and
ebook formats are available online.

Find more titles and sign up to our readers' newsletter at
http://www.johnhuntpublishing.com/mind-body-spirit
Follow us on Facebook at
https://www.facebook.com/OBooks/ and Twitter at
https://twitter.com/obooks